A BIOGRAPHY OF

Lady Bird Johnson

Legacy of Beauty

BY ROSE HOUK

WESTERN NATIONAL PARKS ASSOCIATION | TUCSON, ARIZONA

Acknowledgments

Superintendent David Vela, Sandy Hodges, and staff at the Lyndon B. Johnson National Historical Park provided generous assistance and careful reviews to make this book a reality. Mrs. Johnson's daughter, Lynda Robb, and granddaughter, Catherine Robb, graciously took time to share thoughts of their mother and grandmother. Stewart Udall opened his home for a fascinating interview, and Sharon Francis offered many memories. The good people at the LBJ Library were steadfastly helpful—special thanks to Mrs. Johnson's executive assistant, Shirley James, for her ready responses and wonderful tour of the LBJ ranch, and to archivists Barbara Constable and Claudia Anderson for making research a joyful task. Gratitude goes to Ellen Ahr for her early reading of the manuscript, and to Robert Breunig and Karen Enyedy for recollections and recommendations. Editor Abby Mogollón did an astute job of smoothing the rough edges and asking the right questions.

Copyright © 2006 by Rose Houk
ISBN 10: 1-58369-061-1
ISBN 13: 978-1583690-611
Published by Western National Parks Association
The net proceeds from WNPA publications support educational and research programs in the national parks. Receive a free Western National Parks Association catalog, featuring hundreds of publications. Email: info@wnpa.org or visit www.wnpa.org

Written by Rose Houk
Edited by Abby Mogollón
Designed by Nancy Campana / Campana Design
Photography by: Front cover: C9479-17, LBJ Library Photo by Robert Knudsen; page 3: Willard Clay; page 4: 41-6-84, LBJ Library Photo by Austin Statesman; page 6: B9742, LBJ Library Photo from Taylor Family Collection, photographer unknown; page 8 *(top)*: B6369-5, LBJ Library Photo from Taylor Family Collection, photographer unknown; page 8 *(bottom):* Laurence Parent; page 9: B2684, LBJ Library Photo by unknown; page 10: B7029-3, LBJ Library Photo by unknown; page 12, Laurence Parent; page 13: B9798 LBJ Library Photo by unknown; page 14: B1621-3, LBJ Library Photo by unknown; page 17: B6330-2, LBJ Library Photo from Johnson Family Album, photographer unknown; page 18 *(left):* C5309-4a, LBJ Library Photo by Mike Geissinger; page 18 *(right):* 59-12-91, LBJ Library Photo by Frank Muto; page 20: C9959-23A, LBJ Library Photo by Robert Knudsen; page 22, 1A-1-WH63, LBJ Library Photo by Cecil Stoughton; page 25: 33317, LBJ Library by unknown; page 27: B8626-1, LBJ Library Photo by Yoichi R. Okamoto; page 28-29: Laurence Parent; page 30: C9079-4, LBJ Library Photo by Robert Knudsen, page 32: 33020-13a, LBJ Library Photo by Robert Knudsen; page 33: C1955-32A, LBJ Library Photo by Robert Knudsen; page 34: 34199-13, LBJ Library Photo by unknown; page 36 C1616-9A, LBJ Library Photo by Robert Knudsen; page 37: Willard Clay; page 39: C9284-6, LBJ Library Photo by Yoichi R. Okamoto; page 40: D9233-12, LBJ Library Photo by Frank Wolf; page 42: D4826-6, LBJ Library Photo by Frank Wolf; page 43: Laurence Parent; page 44: D7253-35a, LBJ Library Photo by Frank Wolf.
Printing by Everbest Printing Company, Ltd.
Printed in China

contents

She has been known by many names through her long life: Claudia Alta Taylor at birth, Lady Bird as a child, Bird as a young woman, Mrs. Lyndon Johnson upon her marriage, first lady, and later "Nini" to her grandchildren and great-grandchildren. Each name reflects different chapters in the life of this gracious woman, known best to most people simply as Lady Bird Johnson.

CHILDHOOD PORTRAIT, 1915

Claudia Alta Taylor

S he was a healthy 6 ½-pound baby girl, born early on a Sunday morning, December 22, 1912. Her mother was Minnie Patillo Taylor and father was Thomas Jefferson Taylor. A few weeks later, Thomas Taylor wrote to his wife's sister, Effie, to announce: "Yes *we* have a little girl . . . she really is very pretty and Minnie is *very* proud of her." Her full name was Claudia Alta Taylor, but her nursemaid thought the dark-eyed, fetching baby girl was pretty as a lady bird; thus arose the nickname that's been with her ever since.

The place was Karnack, a small town in deep east Texas, where the Taylors had moved from Alabama. In Karnack, Thomas became a prosperous merchant and landowner; to some he was known as

THE BRICK HOUSE

CADDO LAKE

"Mister Boss" and to others as "Captain Taylor." But Minnie found
little to interest her there. She preferred to visit relatives back in
Alabama, attend the opera in a city, or read books. In 1918, she drove
with her young daughter, Claudia, in the family's Hudson Super Six
to campaign against a candidate for county commissioner. Though
active in the causes she believed in, Minnie suffered from severe
headaches and other health problems. In the same year as that campaign trip, she died, only forty-four years old.

At age five Lady Bird and her two elder brothers were left to be
raised by others. Aunt Effie arrived in Karnack at the Brick House, as
the antebellum plantation home was known. Though Lady Bird's
father soon remarried, it wasn't the stepmother but Aunt Effie who
reared the youngster.

Aunt Effie, who had never married, proved a permissive surrogate parent. Young Lady Bird wandered as she pleased near the home place, barefoot in summer, often alone; one of her favorite spots was Caddo Lake, where blackwater lagoons were lined with cypress trees festooned with Spanish moss. Engrossed in a book or swimming with turtles and alligators, she found companionship in the natural world.

Her aunt taught Lady Bird "how to listen to the wind in the pine trees and to the way birds sing," Mrs. Johnson later wrote. Effie was

LADY BIRD (LEFT) IN AIRPLANE

also the source of adventure. She and her young charge vacationed in Alabama together. In 1923, when Lady Bird was eleven, they traveled as far as Michigan, to the Kellogg Sanitarium where a health regime offered promise for the frail older woman. There, on that Fourth of July holiday, Lady Bird took a thrilling ride in a biplane piloted by a woman.

Always, the Taylor family held education in high regard. Claudia attended the one-room Fern School No. 14 during the elementary years. She went to high schools in the nearby towns of Jefferson and Marshall. In those years she started to shed some shyness, going to dances and on picnics and dates. A rarity among her friends, she had a car of her own—as a teenager, she and another girl drove all the way from Karnack to Alabama by themselves to visit family.

Upon graduation from high school, Lady Bird enrolled in Saint Mary's Episcopal School for Girls, a junior college in Dallas. Her two years there were lonely ones, but she discovered the theater and rediscovered literature, thanks to an English teacher "who made words . . . a source of excitement." During her time at the school, she converted from her Methodist upbringing to the Episcopal Church.

GRADUATION, UNIVERSITY OF TEXAS, 1934

LADY BIRD JOHNSON

Bird

T hen "Bird" (she had succeeded in shortening her childhood nickname) was off to the University of Texas in Austin. She was a good and serious student, but it wasn't all work. For fun, she went out with her good friends Eugenia "Gene" Boehringer and Cecille Harrison. Claudia was "just a delightful young girl," recalled Gene, and "she loved Austin." There were so many interesting things to do and people to meet in the dazzling state capital. Bird always had lots of "beaus." With friends or a date, she visited favorite spots where they would picnic and pose dreamily for pictures in fields blanketed with bluebonnets. Other places offered horses to ride, and Bird was a good horsewoman.

The tall, outgoing Lyndon, then twenty-six years old, was "the most outspoken, straight-forward, determined young man I had ever encountered. I knew I'd met something remarkable, but I didn't quite know what."

"The University was mine during the days of the Depression," recalled Lady Bird. "It seemed then . . . that all of the doors of the world suddenly swung open to me. Here I discovered that college is only the beginning of learnings, and that one new horizon only opens the door to still another."

She received her first bachelor's degree in history in 1933. The following year she returned to the university, where she wrote articles for the college newspaper under the byline Claudia Alta Taylor, and completed studies for a degree in journalism, a possible career.

As a graduation trip that summer, Bird and Cecille Harrison embarked on a long, glamorous trip by boat from the port of Galveston, Texas, to New York City and Washington, D.C. Little did Bird know that the graduation trip was only the beginning of her adventures and travels. As soon as she got back, the horizon of her world was about to tilt in a most dramatic way.

THE DRISKILL HOTEL, AUSTIN

Gene Boehringer had spoken of a young man she wanted Bird to meet. His name was Lyndon Johnson. At the time a legislative secretary to Congressman Richard Kleberg in Washington, Lyndon assuredly was a man on the move. On an August afternoon in 1934 when he was in Austin, Boehringer briefly introduced him to Bird. The next morning he and Bird had breakfast at the Driskill Hotel downtown. As they drove around, Lyndon talked nonstop about his ambitions. By the end of the day he announced his intention to marry her. The next day, he whisked Bird off to meet his parents in the small town of San Marcos, then took her to Kleberg's vast King Ranch. On his way back to Washington, they stopped in Karnack, where Lyndon asked Thomas Taylor for his daughter's hand.

Good friends and her Aunt Effie expressed reservations about the abbreviated courtship, but Bird's father was favorably impressed—as was Lady Bird herself. The tall, outgoing Lyndon, then twenty-six years old, was to her "terribly, terribly interesting" and "the most outspoken, straight-forward, determined young man I had ever encountered. I knew I'd met something remarkable, but I didn't quite know what." Persuasive as only Lyndon Johnson could be, he persuaded Lady Bird with his ardor. On November 17 they were married in a hastily arranged ceremony at an Episcopal church in San Antonio. The next day, Lady Bird called Gene Boehringer and informed her that "Lyndon and I committed matrimony last night." The newlyweds then set off for a honeymoon in Mexico. Claudia Alta Taylor, now Mrs. Lyndon Baines Johnson, was about to embark on a great journey to a fascinating future she could barely have imagined.

MR. AND MRS. JOHNSON
ON THEIR HONEYMOON,
MEXICO, 1934

IN FRONT OF THE CAPITOL, WASHINGTON, D.C., 1934–35

Mrs. Lyndon B. Johnson

I n a letter to Lyndon during their courtship, she had
implored him, "Please tell me as soon as you can what the
deal is . . . . I am *afraid* it is politics . . . . Oh, I know I
haven't any . . . proprietary interest—but I would hate for
you to go into politics."

Her premonition was right, of course. It *was* politics, and Mrs.
Lyndon Johnson would become as familiar with the paths of Congress
as she had been with the bayous of east Texas. She would learn per-
haps more than she wanted to know about that world. She shared in
her husband's rise to power, becoming his trusted advisor.

And, she would discover how to coexist with LBJ's very different
style and pace. Where he was brash, impetuous, and impatient, she

was gentle, thoughtful, and composed. Lady Bird loved the theater, books, and travel. His idea of fun was to head out to his beloved Hill Country, check on the cattle and the deer, and visit with local ranchers and farmers. Yet Mrs. Johnson managed to serve as both his helpmate and partner, loyally supporting his wishes and goals while remaining very much her own person. Of their partnership, she often said: "Lyndon is the catalyst, and I am the amalgam."

For a short time after their wedding, she and Lyndon lived in an apartment in Washington on his meager salary. He kept up a feverish work schedule. His habit of popping in with guests for dinner sent his new wife, who had never spent much time in the kitchen, to her Fannie Farmer cookbook to put passable meals on the table.

In the summer of 1935, Lyndon and Lady Bird moved back to Austin, where he served as state director of the National Youth Administration, a job-creation program. Among the projects was building roadside parks, and as Lady Bird traveled the state with him that idea struck a chord that would resonate for her many years later. It wasn't long, though, before LBJ's career as an elected official started in earnest. In 1937, with the help of a loan from his wife's inheritance from her mother, he won a special election for Texas's Tenth Congressional District seat.

So it was back to Washington, D.C., for the couple. In her diary for February 13, 1941, Mrs. Johnson noted that she attended her first dinner at the White House that night, given for the Duchess of Luxembourg. The women had coffee with "Mrs. R"(Eleanor Roosevelt) in one of the drawing rooms and then went upstairs and watched *The Philadelphia Story.* "Big day!!" wrote Mrs. Johnson in that day's entry. Of course, she could not have known then that she would live in the nation's capital for nearly forty years, the last ones in that awe-inspiring presidential home.

After Pearl Harbor, Lyndon joined the Navy and served in the South Pacific. In his absence Lady Bird ran his congressional office, answering constituent requests and dealing with his staff. It was a test of her administrative prowess, and she measured up quite capably.

In March 1944, Lynda Bird was born, and in 1947 their second daughter, Lucy Baines, arrived.

She came away from the experience confident she could make a living for herself.

At the end of 1942, with Lyndon back from service, Lady Bird put that business acumen into practice. Drawing on her inheritance, the Johnsons bought an Austin radio station, KTBC. It was struggling, but with frugality and hands-on management Mrs. Johnson rebuilt it into a profitable enterprise. Each week she received an envelope containing the station's financial figures, poring over them and making savvy decisions. Said one associate, "she reads a balance sheet like most women examine a piece of cloth."

Yet business and politics weren't enough. Mrs. Johnson desired to own a home and to start a family. She and Lyndon finally bought a house in northwest Washington. And though she had suffered several miscarriages, in 1943 she found she was pregnant again. In March 1944, Lynda Bird was born, and in 1947 their second daughter, Lucy Baines, arrived (Lucy would later change the spelling to Luci). With a Cine-Kodak camera that Lyndon gave her for Christmas, Lady Bird played amateur cinematographer, shooting movies of her children, other family members, her beloved Austin, and Lyndon's campaigns; she even produced humorous vaudeville-type productions, with music

THE JOHNSON FAMILY,
TEXAS, 1948

and her own narration. There was her "Daddy" on the porch of the Brick House in Karnack; Lynda in her first year, squirming in a baby buggy and sunbathing with her mother in the backyard; another with Luci a few weeks old; others featured the girls at birthday parties, dressed in Halloween costumes, and opening Christmas presents.

Although she had two toddlers to tend and was actively involved with the radio station in those years, Mrs. Johnson found time to organize a woman's division to campaign for her husband in his race for the Senate in 1948. She delivered her first stump speeches and then celebrated her husband's slim victory.

In the fall of 1951, LBJ took Lady Bird out to a ranch west of Johnson City, Texas, on the Pedernales River. It belonged to his Aunt Frank, and he told his wife he wanted to buy the house and about 250 acres. Recalling the plan, Lady Bird later told author Ruth Montgomery, "Certainly I remember my reaction to it. It was one of complete withdrawal. I thought, 'Oh, my Lord, no!' We had just gotten the house in Washington a short while before, and I did so love to be there. I knew the old stone ranchhouse would take so much work to fix up. I could hardly bear the thought of it!" Still, she dove into renovating the house and redecorating it with favorite furnishings and keepsakes. Soon she was calling it "our heart's home."

TEXAS WHITE HOUSE, LBJ RANCH, LYNDON B. JOHNSON NATIONAL HISTORICAL PARK
(RIGHT) SENATOR AND MRS. JOHNSON IN 1934 FORD ON PEDERNALES RIVER DAM, LBJ RANCH, 1959

In 1955, only months after he became Senate Majority Leader, LBJ was struck by a serious heart attack. Lady Bird stayed by his side through his months of recovery, a good part of it at the ranch. She tried valiantly, sometimes vainly, to get him to watch his diet, stop smoking, and slow down. His health remained a constant concern to her. On July 2, 1964, even as they celebrated Luci's seventeenth birthday, she noted that "in the background of today there is always present in my mind, and I am sure in Lyndon's mind, the fact that this is the ninth anniversary of his serious heart attack. For the first few years we passed those milestones stepping softly with great trepidation. Now we act almost as though the heart attack had not been, though Lyndon and I will not forget."

Lady Bird faced most of life's challenges head-on, but she harbored a true fear of speaking before an audience. With discipline and determination, she decided to conquer that fear by taking speech lessons. She met regularly with a tutor in 1959, receiving instruction she would soon put to effective use.

In 1960 John F. Kennedy and Lyndon Johnson waged their campaign for president and vice-president. Again, Mrs. Johnson was intimately involved, giving speeches throughout the South, urging women to write, call, and get out the vote. She also traveled nearly 35,000 miles in seventy days, made many solo appearances, and stood beside her husband on more than a hundred occasions—all despite a distressing encounter with a group of protesters in Dallas and the death of her father just before the election.

As wife of the vice-president, Lady Bird kept up an indefatigable schedule, traveling the world with Lyndon. She also started her Women Doers luncheons, choosing an important national issue and inviting professional women to the White House to speak on the topic.

Lady Bird Johnson found herself poised where the events of history would change her life irrevocably.

WHITE HOUSE PORTRAIT, 1968

First Lady

T he Lyndon Baines Johnson Library and Museum in Austin contains an arresting exhibit. It is the clothing that Lady Bird and Lyndon wore the day President John F. Kennedy was assassinated. The two items—his a charcoal gray suit, hers a two-piece white dress— hang spotless and perfectly pressed inside a glass case. Simple and stark, the display serves as a powerful reminder that the Johnsons were there that bright Friday morning in Dallas, riding in a car behind the president's.

Lady Bird begins *A White House Diary* with a recounting of the traumatic events as they unfolded on November 22, 1963. The sharp report of shots, the mad rush to the hospital, her recognition of the

Numb and disbelieving, she said she felt as if she were moving through a Greek tragedy—assuming the role of first lady of the United States, a role for which she had never rehearsed.

NOVEMBER 22, 1963

horrible truth when she saw the face of President Kennedy's aide, Kenny O'Donnell, and heard him utter the words: "The President is dead."

The plan had been for the Kennedys to go to Austin for a fundraiser that evening and continue on to the LBJ Ranch. Everything had been readied for their arrival—the traditional barbecue with entertainment, the phone lines, even a special bed for the president because of his back ailment.

Instead, Mrs. Johnson found herself aboard Air Force One, part of the grim, silent group gathered around her husband as he took the oath of office as the nation's thirty-sixth president. "One of the most poignant sights" during that long flight back to Washington, one that stayed in her mind, was of Jacqueline Kennedy, "that immaculate woman exquisitely dressed, and caked in blood."

At the Capitol two days later, where Kennedy's body lay in state, she wrote: "It was a day I will never forget—nor will the people of America." Numb and disbelieving, she said she felt as if she were moving through a Greek tragedy—assuming the role of first lady of the United States, a role for which she had never rehearsed.

Pressed about when she planned to move into the White House, Mrs. Johnson replied, "I would to God I could serve Mrs. Kennedy's comfort; I can at least serve her convenience." Finally on December 7, carrying the cherished photograph of former House Speaker and friend Sam Rayburn, she made the move to her new home at 1600 Pennsylvania Avenue. The historic mansion with 132 rooms and a staff of seventy-five necessarily dictated a dramatic transformation in Lady Bird's domestic world.

On December 22, her birthday, the official period of mourning ended, the black crepe came down, and Lady Bird Johnson assumed her new position with the grace, dignity, determination, and energy she exhibited in everything she did. Yet she was not filled with elation; instead, she confessed a sense "of how hard the road is going to be and the determination to make these twelve months—eleven or whatever they are—as good as I can."

That Christmas, she and LBJ were back at the ranch in Texas, where life assumed some sense of normalcy—she delivered poinsettias to friends and family and enjoyed a big dinner followed by gifts. But then the first lady prepared for visits from the German head of state and the Joint Chiefs of Staff. The ranch, once a respite from Washington, became the "Texas White House" with all that entailed—high-level meetings, constant media attention, and exhausting entertaining. To her it was anything but restful. But she observed, "somehow, the ranch manages to be restful to Lyndon."

On December 22, her birthday, the official period of mourning ended, the black crepe came down, and Lady Bird Johnson assumed her new position with the grace, dignity, determination, and energy she exhibited in everything she did.

In late August, as the Democratic Convention neared, Lady Bird wrote a personal letter to him on White House stationery. "Beloved," she began, and then noted her honor of his bravery, strength, and patience. "To step out now," she went on, "would be wrong for your country, and I can see nothing but a lonely wasteland for your future. . . ."

Back in Washington, D.C., at the start of the new year, Mrs. Johnson escorted the women of the press corps through the White House. She won them over with her attention to their needs and deadlines, along with capable help from her press secretary, friend and seasoned reporter Liz Carpenter.

As first lady, Mrs. Johnson saw her days filled with an endless round of luncheons, dinners, receptions, parties, ceremonies, meetings, and travel. With her social secretary, Bess Abell, by her side, she worked in her office on the second floor of the East Wing, ensuring that the right people were invited to various functions, answering mountains of correspondence and requests for appearances, and following her husband's favored bills through Congress.

The most pressing question that summer, however, was whether LBJ would run for president. He voiced his inner doubts about the wisdom of entering the race to a few close staff members and to his wife. In late August, as the Democratic Convention neared, Lady Bird wrote a personal letter to him on White House stationery. "Beloved," she began, and then noted her honor of his bravery, strength, and patience. "To step out now," she went on, "would be wrong for your country, and I can see nothing but a lonely wasteland for your future . . . ." In conclusion, she counseled that "in the final analysis I can't carry any of the burdens you talked of—so I know it's only your choice." She signed the letter, "I love you always, Bird." On August 27, 1964, Lyndon Johnson accepted his party's nomination for president.

Wasting no time, Mrs. Johnson set into motion plans for an ambitious campaign train tour she would make in October across the

South. She invited every senator and governor of the states she would visit to join her on board, but knew some would decline because of the recent passage of the Civil Rights Act. The law, called the most important civil rights legislation in the nation's history, assured equal rights for all Americans regardless of race, color, religion, and national origin, and it prohibited discrimination in any public accommodations. As president, Lyndon Johnson brought everything he had to bear to achieve its successful passage. But many in the South, even some in Johnson's own party, were not ready to acknowledge or accept desegregation. Though keenly aware of racial tensions, Lady Bird wanted the people to know of her pride in and love of the South. "For me," she said, "it is going to be a journey of the heart."

Dubbed the "Lady Bird Special," the whistlestop train tour made more than forty stops in eight states in four very full days. One of the nineteen cars was refurbished in snappy red, white, and blue, serving as the hospitality car, complete with a bevy of Southern belles as hostesses. From the platform of the caboose Mrs. Johnson waved to the

WHISTLESTOP TOUR,
1964 PRESIDENTIAL
CAMPAIGN

Of that time, said Lynda, "She was my best friend, you could tell her your secrets." Luci expressed a wish for more time with her mother, but at the same time realized that she received something as important: "our greatest inheritance . . . two parents who adored each other. . . . "

crowds, delivered brief speeches, and accepted uncounted bouquets of yellow roses. Daughters Lynda and Luci joined at stops along the way, and at the end of the line in New Orleans, a beaming LBJ arrived.

Lyndon Johnson won his race against Republican Barry Goldwater in 1964, yet Lady Bird felt vaguely let down afterwards. She confessed to her diary on November 17, the date of her thirtieth wedding anniversary, that she could not seem to shake "a curious pall of sadness and inertia," a feeling of having come to a standstill due to the Vietnam War and other serious problems facing the nation and her husband. But that evening her spirits were lifted considerably by a surprise party Lyndon gave for her.

Such moments of doubt or gloominess were rare for Lady Bird Johnson, who normally displayed an unbridled optimism and self-confidence. It was unusual when she could not move herself to work, for that was a value she held in highest esteem—embodied in a small plaque on her desk inscribed with the words "Can Do."

She spoke almost with guilt of stealing time for "indulgences"— reading in bed, playing bridge, going bowling or swimming, watching "Gunsmoke" on Saturday night, or enjoying time at the ranch. Yet she realized that "the tempo of life must be slow sometime for you to really savor its moments." Mrs. Johnson also recognized the "precious balance" between a woman's "domestic and civic life." With all the incumbent duties of a loyal politician's wife and first lady, she often was compelled to practice that balancing act. She had plenty of able help, with people like Willie Day Taylor keeping track of Lynda and Luci, and longtime cook Zephyr Wright preparing meals. Mrs. Johnson relished times when Lynda whisked her away to a museum or a concert, and she saw Luci through high school graduation and her baptism into the Catholic Church. Both daughters were married during the White House years, and each gave Mrs. Johnson a grand-child in those years. Of that time, said Lynda, "She was my best friend, you could tell her your secrets." Luci expressed a wish for more time with her mother, but at the same time realized that she received something as important: "our greatest inheritance. . . . two parents who adored each other. . . We may not have always had our parents there, but we always had that foundation."

(LEFT TO RIGHT) LYNDA BIRD JOHNSON, LUCI BAINES JOHNSON, LYNDON BAINES JOHNSON, AND LADY BIRD JOHNSON, 1963

DECEMBER 22, 1912

Born in Karnack, Texas

| November 17, 1934 marries Lyndon B. Johnson | 1942 manages LBJ's congressional office while he serves in World War II, purchases Austin radio station KTBC | MARCH 19, 1944 first child, Lynda Bird Johnson, born | JULY 2, 1947 Luci Baines Johnson born | 1961 Mrs. Johnson becomes second lady of the United States | NOVEMBER 22, 1963 President John F. Kennedy assassinated, Mrs. Johnson becomes first lady |

1964
passage of national Civil Rights Act, Mrs. Johnson campaigns on the "Lady Bird Special"

OCTOBER 22, 1965
Federal Highway Beautification Act becomes law

1970
publication of *A White House Diary*

1972
with her husband, donates the LBJ Ranch house and surrounding property near Stonewall, Texas, as national historic site; LBJ Library and Museum opens

JANUARY 22, 1973
Lyndon B. Johnson dies

DECEMBER 22, 1982
National Wildflower Research Center opens, later renamed the Lady Bird Johnson Wildflower Center

LADY BIRD JOHNSON VISITS CLASSROOM FOR PROJECT HEAD START, 1968

Lady Bird Johnson

A s first lady, Mrs. Johnson decided to focus on a few things that sparked her interest, rather than dilute her efforts across too many fronts. Children and their education surfaced as one priority. Hence, she became the first honorary chair of Project Head Start, a program to prepare preschoolers of low-income families for the classroom, part of her husband's Great Society and War on Poverty efforts. "Our hope," explained Mrs. Johnson, "was to rescue the next generation—there were thousands of children who became dropouts in the third and fourth grade." To see recipients of the program firsthand, she visited schools in Newark, New Jersey, and elsewhere in the country.

But the cause to which she devoted most attention, the one for which she is most remembered, was "beautification." It was a label Mrs. Johnson never fully embraced—to her it conveyed something cosmetic and trivial and failed to describe the true breadth of her vision.

"Getting on the subject of beautification," she observed, "is like picking up a tangled skein of wool—all the threads are interwoven—recreation and pollution and mental health, and the crime rate, and rapid transit, and highway beautification, and the war on poverty, and parks. . . . It is hard to hitch the conversation into one straight line, because everything leads to something else."

Alas, neither she nor anyone else ever came up with a better word. As time went on, people began to appreciate that beautification encompassed much more than planting flowers, picking up litter, or removing roadside billboards. For Lady Bird it embraced larger conservation efforts, and occasionally, the coming trend of environmentalism. Clearly, it grew out of her childhood affinity for nature and extended as a deeply held passion into adulthood.

WITH STEWART UDALL, GRAND TETON NATIONAL PARK, 1964

As first lady, in partnership with the president, she elevated the topic to a top rung on the national agenda. During 1964 she began to develop a partnership with Secretary of the Interior Stewart Udall, who would work with her throughout the White House years. Udall warmly recalled a "special relationship" with her, adding, "if I had Lady Bird's support that gave me a lift up" in convincing others.

That summer she toured the western United States with Udall, including a visit to the Crow Reservation in Montana and the Grand

Tetons in Wyoming. They took a float trip on the Snake River—it was "billed as a conservation trip," he remembered, and "she loved it." In Udall's mind that excursion proved a crucible: "I think on that first trip that she decided that preserving the beauty of the country was going to be her project." On the flight back, Mrs. Johnson sat with him and "she just talked and talked about what the [Interior] department was trying to do, our programs, she was asking questions . . . she wanted to know everything."

Lyndon Johnson's State of the Union address in January 1965 won his wife's stamp of approval for his "accent" on education, medical research, and preserving the nation's beauty. Especially, she was pleased with the emphasis on beauty—for America's highways,

LADY BIRD JOHNSON DEDICATES WATTS BRANCH PARK, 1966

Getting on the subject of beautification," she observed, "is like picking up a tangled skein of wool—all the threads are interwoven—recreation and pollution and mental health, and the crime rate, and rapid transit, and highway beautification, and the war on poverty, and parks. . . . It is hard to hitch the conversation into one straight line, because everything leads to something else."

cities, and national parks. "I hope we can do something about that in our four years here," she vowed.

Right away, she formed the Committee for a More Beautiful Capital. Meeting each month at the White House, the group aimed to beautify Mrs. Johnson's "hometown" of Washington, D.C., turning it into a model city for the nation and the world. She was receiving so much mail on the subject that Stewart Udall detailed an assistant, Sharon Francis, to help draft responses. Francis soon worked full-time with the first lady, and along with Cynthia Wilson, served as a key aide on beautification and conservation matters.

Along with Udall, National Park Service Regional Director Nash Castro, and the city's mayor, Walter Washington, the Committee for a More Beautiful Capital also included influential philanthropists, among them Mary Lasker, Laurance Rockefeller, and Mrs. Vincent Astor. They contributed money and influence, donating or raising handsome sums for daffodil and tulip bulbs, azaleas, and cherry trees. Mrs. Johnson would then set out with shovel or trowel, digging the first hole in the ground of a traffic triangle, a park, or a school play-ground in the city. "We lost count of how many trees Mrs. Johnson had planted after the fifty-fourth, a dogwood," quipped Liz Carpenter.

PLANTING CHERRY TREES,
WASHINGTON, D.C., 1965

As she confided, "I am a natural born tourist, an adventurer . . . and I fell in love all over again with the physical country."

Lady Bird "wanted hands-on accomplishments, she wanted on the ground to see things happen," commented Sharon Francis. Not infrequently Mrs. Johnson would announce "let's go out for a drive," and off they went for a look at a newly landscaped site or a housing project playground in parts of Washington where tourists didn't go.

Whenever possible, Mrs. Johnson ventured out to see more of the country. Whether a courthouse square, a presidential home, or a remote wilderness, she savored the opportunity. As she confided, "I am a natural born tourist, an adventurer . . . and I fell in love all over again with the physical country."

That enthusiasm, plus the accompanying beneficial publicity, led to some highly visible trips while she was first lady. An early, notable jaunt was the Landscapes and Landmarks tour in the spring of 1965. Nash Castro, loyal sidekick during those beautification days, had done advance work for the trip and was among the entourage of seventy people. They traveled by bus, stopping along Interstate 95 where Mrs. Johnson put a plant in the ground, lunching at Thomas Jefferson's Monticello, and ending on the Blue Ridge Parkway. While *Life* and *Saturday Evening Post* photographers took shots of the first lady back-dropped by the mountains, she was snapping their pictures too. Wherever she went and whenever she spoke, people were captivated, said Castro. What Lady Bird so clearly projected, he observed, was "her deep, deep interest in enhancing the beauty of the country."

The White House Conference on Natural Beauty took place soon after, in May. Mrs. Johnson opened the meeting and studiously took notes as she sat in on panels. The conference provided a forum that reinforced high-level support for her beautification programs—and participants delivered reports directly to President Johnson for tangible actions.

With the president's backing, Congress soon set to work on a package of bills to regulate billboards on the nation's highways. The Highway Beautification bill generated a real political battle. On many trips between Texas and Washington, Mrs. Johnson had been disturbed by unsightly billboards, unscreened junkyards, and litter

MRS. JOHNSON (WEARING COWBOY HAT) LEADING HIKERS ON LOST MINE TRAIL, CHISOS MOUNTAINS, BIG BEND NATIONAL PARK, 1966

along the roadsides. So when "Lady Bird's bill" was introduced, she acted as a full player in the effort to get it passed. She applied her considerable powers of persuasion on members of Congress but faced an equally strong lobby in the outdoor advertising industry. The bill became law on October 22, 1965. Although it didn't go as far as Lady Bird or others wished, it was a start, and some observers considered her active role in the law's passage historic for a first lady.

In April 1966 Mrs. Johnson set off on another well-publicized trip—a splashy one this time. She went to Big Bend National Park way out in west Texas on the Rio Grande. Along on this and several other trips was National Park Service Director George Hartzog. When they arrived at the park and were about to have lunch, Hartzog motioned Mrs. Johnson to stand, whereupon she awarded him a check for her park entry pass. The large group then took a hike into the Chisos Mountains, and Mrs. Johnson couldn't resist poking a little fun: "Into the wilderness of these majestic towering crags—this

The large group then took a hike into the Chisos Mountains, and Mrs. Johnson couldn't resist poking a little fun: "Into the wilderness of these majestic towering crags—this eons-old graphic story of the geological history of the earth, this solitude—thundered the motley crew of one hundred."

eons-old graphic story of the geological history of the earth, this solitude—thundered the motley crew of one hundred." The itinerary also
included a cookout under the full moon, mariachi music, and an outdoor church service on Palm Sunday. The crowd then set out for the
river where twenty-four rafts—"quite an armada" observed Nash
Castro—launched on a daylong float. One of the press women sported
a red parasol and red pants, another wore a polka-dot bikini. A more
sedately dressed first lady rode in the bow of a boat. Looking up at the
sheer canyon walls, her face showed complete rapture and delight.

On one of her last big trips as first lady, Mrs. Johnson journeyed to
northern California in the fall of 1968 to dedicate the new Redwood
National Park. It had been a long-fought effort to save the last remaining stands of the grand old trees. She was honored by the naming of
one group of fine specimens the Lady Bird Johnson Grove. As she
walked among the redwoods, dressed in beige slacks and jacket and hat,
Mrs. Johnson was "in her glory," said Nash Castro, "she was radiant."

LADY BIRD JOHNSON GROVE,
REDWOOD NATIONAL PARK,
CALIFORNIA

In her dedication speech at the new park, Mrs. Johnson proclaimed that "the gift of the redwoods is peace." By the time she gave that speech, she was ready to accept that gift. Several months earlier, on March 31, Lyndon Johnson had shocked the nation with a live televised speech announcing his decision not to run for re-election. The Vietnam War was growing more divisive each day, and Mrs. Johnson's spirit was saddened and wearied by it. She made it clear she did not want to endure another campaign, and always she harbored that deep-seated fear for her husband's health. Again the final decision was up to him. In his speech Lyndon Johnson said to her and to the nation: "I do not believe that I should devote an hour or a day of my time to any personal partisan causes or to any other duties than the awesome duties of this office. . . . Accordingly, I shall not seek—and I will not accept—the nomination of my party for another term as your President." Lady Bird rejoined, "We have done a lot; there's a lot left to do in the remaining months; maybe this is the only way to get it done."

Conditions in the nation worsened with the assassinations of Martin Luther King in April and Robert Kennedy in June. Cities were in flames, and society appeared at the breaking point. Still, Lady Bird Johnson kept at her conservation work, counting the days until they would leave Washington for their beloved ranch in Texas.

On January 19, 1969, she and Lyndon had a "last supper" with family and friends, saying their goodbyes and thank-yous. The following day Mrs. Johnson wrote in her diary that she awoke early, and in her robe with a cup of coffee in hand, went through the rooms of the

On January 19, 1969, she and Lyndon had a "last supper" with family and friends, saying their goodbyes and thank-yous. The following day Mrs. Johnson wrote in her diary that she awoke early, and in her robe with a cup of coffee in hand, went through the rooms of the White House one last time, "mostly just to stand still and absorb the feeling. . . ."

White House one last time, "mostly just to stand still and absorb the feeling. . . ." She dressed, put on her mink hat and muff, and stepped into the limousine that would take her to the Capitol to attend Richard Nixon's inauguration. Looking back, she saw staff members standing on the steps, "smiling and blowing kisses. . . .That was my last view as I drove away."

Back in Texas that night, headed for the ranch, she wrote, "I looked over my shoulder and there was a silver crescent of a new moon, bright and clear and full of promise."

PARTNERS IN THE WHITE HOUSE, MARCH 1968

LADY BIRD AT THE LBJ RANCH, 1991

Nini

Once back home, Mrs. Johnson kept the beautification light burning. She launched a program to honor Texas Highway Department workers for their efforts planting native wildflowers and maintaining roadside parks. She appreciated the people who actually got things done, and it was on them that she lavished commendation. She was also appointed to the National Park Service Advisory Board in 1969.

Meanwhile, Lady Bird was devoting many hours to her book, *A White House Diary*. A few days after the Kennedy assassination, she began to recount daily events into a tape recorder. During her five years as first lady she recorded some 1.7 million words; the diary, published in 1970, represented about one-seventh of the material. In producing it, she came away with "a deep, roaring faith in and love for this country." The book furnishes an invaluable personal record of the first lady's activities and thoughts; more, it reveals a bigger picture of a historic time of transition and tumult in the nation.

Mrs. Johnson also pursued another project that she and LBJ had begun during their White House days—creating the Lyndon Baines Johnson Presidential Library and Museum on the University of Texas campus in Austin. The library officially opened in 1971. Among the holdings are some forty-five million pages of historical documents relating to the president and Mrs. Johnson, plus an enormous audio-visual collection. On the tenth floor of the library/museum is the First Lady's Gallery. In one window-filled corner, Mrs. Johnson's office has been reproduced in every detail—eyeglasses on the desktop, sweater draped over her chair, the couch upholstered in her favorite color—bright coral.

During the early 1970s, Lady Bird also served six years on the University of Texas Board of Regents. Though she wasn't inclined to accept the position, she did so at her husband's urging, and the job became a great point of pride for her. On January 22, 1973, she had gone, again at his urging, to a regents meeting in Austin. That day, Lyndon Johnson died.

LADY BIRD AND LYNDON,
LBJ RANCH, 1972

Both of them knew his heart was failing. He'd had renewed attacks of painful angina, and he used oxygen to help his breathing. But on that January morning, "to my lasting regret" said Mrs. Johnson, he was alone. LBJ had taken a drive around the ranch, eaten lunch, and gone for an afternoon nap. A Secret Service agent received the frantic radio call from the former president, but by the time he got there Lyndon lay unconscious in his bedroom. He was pronounced dead at a San Antonio hospital. Lady Bird flew there, and upon receiving the news said in sad resignation, "Well, we expected it, didn't we?" She and Lyndon had gotten to spend four years and two days together at the ranch after the presidency. For that, and all their years together, she reacted characteristically: "Wouldn't I be ungracious not to be terribly grateful for thirty-eight wonderful years?"

Though she grieved for her husband, Lady Bird moved on. Work was her salvation. She took on several projects near and dear to her heart. One was spearheading development of a hiking and biking trail along Town Lake on the Colorado River in Austin. But her greatest accomplishment was creation of the National Wildflower Research Center. Even as a young child, Lady Bird Johnson loved flowers. She marked the blooming of the first daffodil each spring: "I'd have a little ceremony, and name it the queen." She's planted acres of the ranch grounds with bluebonnets, invited botanists out for flower walks, persuaded crews not to mow the roadsides, and waved down farmers on their tractors to ask about leasing their land just to harvest wildflower

LADY BIRD JOHNSON WITH HER GRANDCHILDREN, LBJ RANCH, 1980

seed. One day during a dry spring she came upon a hillside solid pink with evening primrose. "You could hardly even look at it without wanting to pray or sing or shout," she exclaimed.

On December 22, 1982, Lady Bird Johnson's seventieth birthday, she realized a cherished dream: opening the National Wildflower Research Center in Austin. She and actress Helen Hayes cofounded the center, with Mrs. Johnson donating the land and start-up money. The center's stated mission is to educate people about the environmental necessity, economic value, and natural beauty of native plants. At the dedication Mrs. Johnson threw her straw hat into the air and declared: "I decided to pay my rent for the space I've taken up in this land, and for the pleasure and peace and sustenance this green earth has given me for so many years."

Outgrowing the original location, the center moved to 180 acres on the southern edge of Austin in 1995, and in 1998 it was rededicated and renamed the Lady Bird Johnson Wildflower Center. Stonework architecture, native plant gardens, and walking paths through "living laboratories" create a strong sense of place among the stout live oak and chalky limestone hills of central Texas. Mrs. Johnson takes a keen interest in the center's operations—she's been known to stage spontaneous visits, checking on what's blooming and sharing her carefully kept records of rainfall.

In 1992, on her eightieth birthday, Lady Bird was feted with publication of *A Life Well-Lived,* by Harry Middleton, now former director of the LBJ Library. The volume contains photographs and selected quotations from family and friends, "memories and tributes . . . lodged in hearts of all who know and admire and love this remarkable woman." By that time, Mrs. Johnson was losing her eyesight due to macular degeneration. A reader all her life, she turned to books on tape. She confided to an interviewer that she began listening to birdsong and taking an interest in the clouds, "buttermilk mare's tails." In her eighty-ninth year, Lady Bird Johnson suffered a stroke that left her unable to speak but still able to communicate. She goes out to dinner with her family and friends, visits the wildflower center and Town Lake, enjoys movies, and faithfully watches her favorite nightly news show.

She makes her home in Austin and visits the ranch on weekends and holidays. Her daughters, their husbands, seven grandchildren, and nine great-grandchildren are her delight. She's taken each grand-child on a trip of her or his choosing and has taught them that they have an obligation to do something worthwhile in the world. She remains the source of advice and wisdom for them as they make their own life decisions.

The ranch house is relaxed and lived in, furnished with comfort-able chairs, needlepoint pillows, paintings, a piano, copper pieces from her many travels, the ever-present photograph of Sam Rayburn, and a porch with rocking chairs where Mrs. Johnson likes to greet people. Her bedroom faces out onto her garden, and on her bed are two pillows—one embroidered with "I slept and dreamed that life was beauty," the other "I awoke and found that life was duty." In the din-ing room she sits at the head of the table and wants everyone to listen when one person has something to say. An entire wall of the kitchen is covered with photos of the grandkids with "Nini," as they call her. At gatherings the family plays wicked rounds of a card game called "Onze" (Lady Bird rarely loses), drives out to see the deer or flowers, or walks down to the cemetery. "To us," said granddaughter Catherine Robb, "she *is* the ranch."

"You really have to plan for the future when you plant live oaks," she observed. "But the future is going to happen. If you've got children and grandchildren, you're much more spurred on to plan for the future."

Over the past four decades, Lady Bird Johnson has been recognized with numerous awards for her years of public service, conservation, and humanitarian work—the Eleanor Roosevelt Golden Candlestick Award, the Medal of Freedom, and the Congressional Gold Medal among them—with an additional long list of lifetime achievement awards. She has accepted them all with customary grace, dignity, and humility.

The many awards honor a wide, rich legacy. Lady Bird Johnson has broken new ground in many ways. As first lady, she took unprecedented steps to raise citizens' awareness of the value of their environment and the nation's scenic resources. With the momentum she provided, people beautified their own neighborhoods. On the larger scene, significant new national parks, national seashores, wild and scenic rivers, and wilderness areas were established during the Johnson years, along with enlargement of the Land and Water Conservation Fund. Said National Park Service Director George Hartzog, "She lit a fire in this country that still burns."

Historian Lewis Gould, chronicler of her conservation role, concluded that Lady Bird Johnson "deserves a place with Rachel Carson among the leaders of the impressive company of American women who have imparted first to conservation and later to environmentalism more of its energy and substance than men have recognized." For Mrs. Johnson, sufficient reward would be hearing people appreciate the daffodils in full bloom in Washington, D.C., in the springtime, or having her epitaph read, "She planted three trees."

Although she likely would not call herself a feminist, Lady Bird

Johnson visibly promoted and encouraged women's leadership and public service abilities. By quiet example, she has shown great strength and capacity for growth. She has made sacrifices with a sense of humor and a generous spirit. Even amid an unending glare of publicity she has remained a calm and loyal wife, mother, and friend. Liz Carpenter paid this touching tribute to her: "She's a woman you turn to in times of trouble for comfort and reassurance. . . . Even after the White House years, thousands of letters poured in. They turned to her because they knew she would understand and care. She did and she let them know it."

Another legacy stems from her desire to keep her husband's memory alive. Each August 27 Mrs. Johnson marks his birth with a wreath-laying at his grave in the Johnson family cemetery near the ranch house. In addition, in 1972 she and Lyndon donated a large part of their ranch to the then Lyndon B. Johnson National Historic Site, which already included his birthplace and boyhood home. They did not want the ranch to "become a sterile relic of the past," but instead to remain a working, living place for the rest of their lives. Today, the national historical park operates in close cooperation with the Lyndon B. Johnson State Park and Historic Site that adjoins the ranch property. Lady Bird has remained actively involved in park planning and has been known to cordially greet busloads of visitors when she's outside the ranch house.

Her personal legacy rests in her family—her children, grandchildren, and great-grandchildren. They fuel a faith in Mrs. Johnson, much the same faith required when one plants a slow-growing tree. "You really have to plan for the future when you plant live oaks," she observed. "But the future is going to happen. If you've got children and grandchildren, you're much more spurred on to plan for the future." And like one of those great live oaks of her native Texas, Lady Bird Johnson's legacy of beauty grows deep and strong.

Carpenter, Liz. *Ruffles and Flourishes.* Doubleday, Garden City. 1970.

Gould, Lewis L. *Lady Bird Johnson: Our Environmental First Lady.* University
Press of Kansas, Lawrence. 1988, 1999.

Johnson, Lady Bird. *A White House Diary.* Holt, Rinehart and Winston, New
York. 1970.

Johnson, Lady Bird, and Carlton B. Lees. *Wildflowers Across America.*
National Wildflower Research Center and Abbeville Press,
New York. 1988.

Middleton, Harry. *A Life Well-Lived: Lady Bird Johnson.* The Lyndon Baines
Johnson Foundation, Austin. 1992.

Montgomery, Ruth. *Mrs. LBJ.* Avon Books, New York. 1964.

Letters, speeches, and home movies by Lady Bird Johnson; interviews with
her; transcripts of oral histories from Bess Abell, Nash Castro, Sharon
Francis, Eugenia Boehringer Lasseter, Cecille Harrison Marshall, Dorris
Odum Powell, Anthony Taylor, and Zephyr Wright, all housed in the LBJ
Library in Austin, Texas.

Films, including "Lady Bird Johnson," Southwest Parks and Monuments
Association, 1997; CSPAN interview with Lady Bird Johnson by Brian Lamb,
1999; "Lady Bird Naturally," KLRN-TV, San Antonio, 2001.